Contents

Why do doctors and scientists need this little flower?

Go to page 15 to find out!

What huge animal is this little hyrax closely related to?

Turn to page 31 to find out!

Some words are shown in bold, **like this.** These words are explained in the glossary. You will find important information and definitions underlined, <u>like this</u>.

Classification of animals

There are a huge number of living things on Earth. There are flying fish and swimming birds. There are whales that are bigger than a school bus and bugs that are smaller than the tip of a pin. There are millions of **species** (group of creatures that can breed with each other) of animals living on Earth. So how do scientists group and name all these animals?

Classification

Classification is the method used to group and name animals and other living things. Scientists study millions of species of animals. They need to be able to divide all these animals into smaller groups. Scientists decide what group an animal belongs to by looking at the different parts of the creature. They look at the way it moves, what it eats, and what kind of skin it has. They consider where it lives, what kind of home it needs, and how it acts. They use these features to determine what group a living thing belongs to.

The language of classification

Taxonomy is the science of classification. It includes a special language for naming animals. This language allows scientists to name millions of species of animals.

For example, classification allows scientists to group and name the many species of cat. There are 36 known species of wild cats. The Siberian tiger is the largest of these species. They can reach lengths of 190–220 centimetres (75–79 inches) and weights of 318 kilograms (700 pounds).

Classification helps scientists determine where flying fish and swimming birds should be grouped.

What is classified?

♦ All living things are classified.
♦ Even extinct animals are classified.

Linnaeus' classification system

The **Linnaean classification system** is a popular system of classification for grouping and naming animals. It groups all animals into seven categories It gives each animal a name, known as a scientific name. This system was invented by Swedish scientist Carl Linnaeus (1707–1778). Even though it was invented hundreds of years ago, it is still used by scientists today!

The 7 levels of classification

The Linnaean classification system has seven levels of classification. These are the names scientists give to the levels:

- Kingdom
- Phylum
- Class
- Order
- Family
- Genus
- Species

general

specific

An easy way to remember the groups of taxonomy is the phrase: **K**eep **P**lates **C**lean **O**r **F**amily **G**ets **S**ick. (Kingdom, Phylum, Class, Order, Family, Genus, Species)

In this system, kingdom is the highest category. It is not very specific. In fact, all animals belong to one kingdom, the **Animalia kingdom**, or animal kingdom. Each level below kingdom, from **phylum** to species, is a division of the level above it. Each level is more and more specific. The species level is the most specific. It always includes only one species or type of animal.

Did you know?

There are over 6 billion people alive today. And there are 6,500 languages spoken in 200 different countries. How do scientists from all over the world communicate about all of the species of animals in their countries? The Linnaean classification system provides a universal language of classification. It allows scientists everywhere to communicate about animals from every corner of the world.

Carl Linnaeus wrote over 180 books on classifying different species.

Linnaean grouping

Animals are grouped into the seven categories based on similarities. Let's look at a few examples.

7 levels of human classification

Like all **organisms**, humans are classified into the seven levels of classification. These levels go from very general to very specific. Look at how each level, from kingdom to species, has fewer and fewer different species in it. As each level gets more specific, fewer and fewer animals are included.

The classification of humans			
	Group	**What it includes**	**Approximate number of non-extinct species in group**
Kingdom	Animalia	All animals	>1 million
Phylum	Chordata	Animals with similar body plan or organization	52,000
Class	Mammalia	Chordata with sweat glands and **neocortex region** (part of the brain that only mammals have)	5,400
Order	Primates	Mammalia with collar bone, opposable (moveable) thumbs, other features	350
Family	Hominidae	Primates with capacity for language	4
Genus	*Homo*	Modern humans and extinct human ancestors	1 (many more extinct)
Species	*sapiens*	Modern humans only	1

KEY
> = greater than
< = less than

A lobster is not closely related to the dog or wolf.

Similar and different species

Very similar animals are considered to be closely related. These animals will be grouped together. Animals that are not as closely related will not be grouped together. Remember all animals are in the animal kingdom. However, depending on how similar or different animals are they may not share the same grouping at other levels.

Look at these three species. The red wolf and dog are closely related. They are in the same kingdom, phylum, **class**, **order**, **family**, and **genus**. The lobster isn't similar to the dog or the red wolf. It does not share the same groupings with the dog and red wolf.

	Dog	Red wolf	Lobster
Kingdom	Animalia	Animalia	Animalia
Phylum	Chordata	Chordata	Arthropoda
Class	Mammalia	Mammalia	Malacostraca
Order	Carnivora	Carnivora	Decapoda
Family	Canidae	Canidae	Nephropidae
Genus	*Canis*	*Canis*	*Homarus*
Species	*familiaris*	*rufus*	*Americanus*

Linnaean naming

In the Linnaean system every species of animal is given a two-part name. The name is based on the bottom two levels of classification, genus and species. This is the scientific name.

A first and last name

All animals are given a first and last name just like you have. The first part of the name is a broader, shared name. This is similar to your surname, which you share with your family. The second part is a more specific name. It is not shared. It is like your first name. The shared first part of the name is created from the genus. The specific second part is created from the species.

Linnaeus in Latin

When Linnaeus was alive, Latin was the accepted language of the sciences. Linnaeus used Latin to name the genus and species of many organisms. The name he gave to humans is *Homo sapiens*. *Homo sapiens* is Latin for "wise man". The names Linnaeus gave were descriptive of the organism.

Panthera tigris. The *Panthera* genus includes many species of large cats including the lion and tiger.

Naming animals

Below is a list of some common animals with their scientific names listed first. Notice that the first name (the genus name) is always capitalized and the second name (the species name) is never capitalized. Both are always written in *italics*.

- *Canis familiaris* – dog
- *Panthera leo* – lion
- *Felis domesticus* – cat
- *Panthera tigris* – tiger

Can you tell which of the species above are most closely related? Yes! It is the lion and the tiger. They both begin with *Panthera*. This means that they are both grouped in the same genus, the *Panthera* genus. They are very closely related.

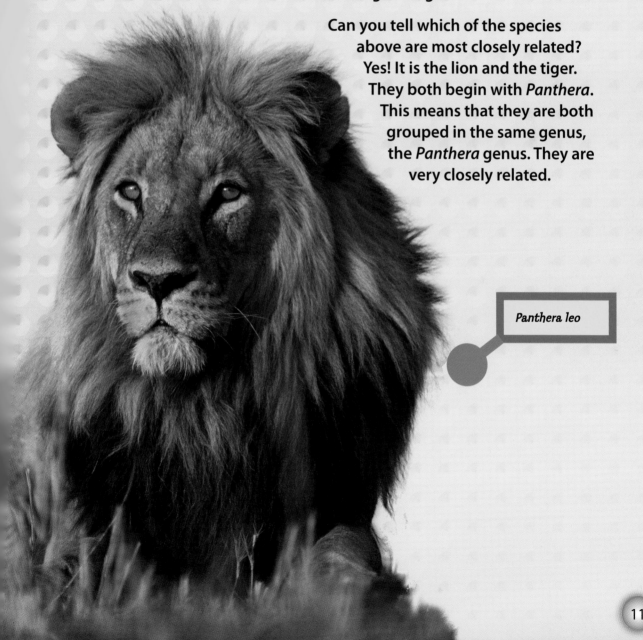

Panthera leo

THE KINGDOMS

The **kingdom** is the highest level in the **Linnaean classification** system. When Linnaeus developed his system, there were only two types of kingdoms: the **plant** and **animal kingdom**. However, microscopes and other technology led to the discovery of many new **organisms** that did not fit in either the plant or animal kingdom. Today there are six kingdoms.

Did you know?

Over 99 per cent of all known species are smaller than a bumblebee. Scientists have named millions of species already, but some scientists estimate there are millions more we don't even know about yet!

If you want to find a new species, think small! There are thought to be millions of species of **eubacteria** (kingdom of tiny organisms) yet to be named.

Grouping into kingdoms

Organisms are grouped into kingdoms mainly according to their cell type, the number of cells in their body, and their ability to make food. Cells are the tiny building blocks that make up all living things. Remember that the kingdom is a very broad category. Each kingdom contains many **species**, some of which may not look very similar at all. An elephant and a snail are both part of the animal kingdom.

Kingdom	Estimated number of known species
Archaea	<300
Eubacteria	>4,000
Protists	>80,000
Fungi	>72,000
Plants	>300,000
Animalia	>1,300,000
Total number of known species	>1,750,000
Possible number of unknown species	5,000,000–100,000,000

KEY
> = **greater than**
< = **less than**

Even though **algae** are tiny and simple organisms, they can create huge problems! To prepare for the 2008 Summer Olympic Games, thousands of people worked to clean up the algae in the rivers around Beijing in China. Algae are part of the protist kingdom.

Archaea kingdom

These **single-celled organisms** (living things made up of only one cell) live without oxygen! They are found in extreme environments, such as hot springs, sea vents (hole in an ocean or sea floor that releases very hot water) and areas deep beneath the soil. They are so tiny that 1,000 of them could fit on the tip of a pin!

Archaea can be found in hot springs like this one.

Eubacteria kingdom

Scientists believe that **bacteria** were the first living things on Earth. Each bacterium is capable of all life functions, such as breathing, eating, and reproduction. Some bacteria can be harmful to humans, like streptococci that cause strep throat. But some are helpful, like those that produce vitamins and yoghurt.

Protist kingdom

This kingdom is made up of both animal-like and plant-like cells.

- Algae are plant-like. They can make their own food from carbon dioxide and sunlight.
- **Protozoa** are animal-like. They can't make their own food. They are found in wet environments.

Lichens are a type of fungus that soak up poisons. When poison levels are high, lichens start to die. This alerts scientists there is a lot of pollution in the area.

Fungi kingdom

Mould, mushrooms, and mildew are **fungi**. Some fungi grow on other plants and animals. They benefit by living on or in a host organism and can be harmful to their host. However, most fungi get food from dead plants or animals. They are the recyclers of life.

Plant kingdom

Plants are **multi-cellular** (have more than one cell) and are made up of complex cells. They do not move from place to place. They have strong cell walls made of **cellulose**. They are also **autotrophs**. This means they make their own food. Life on Earth could not exist without plants.

The Rosy Periwinkle plant is a main ingredient in medicine to treat cancer.

Animal kingdom

The animal kingdom is the largest kingdom, with over 1 million diverse species. Animals cannot make their own food. They must move to find it. They are made up of many cells, which make up different types of **tissue**. Tissues form **organs** such as the heart, the brain, and the lungs. Organs carry out complex jobs.

A KEY TO CLASSIFYING

A key is a tool that can be used by scientists to help them classify an **organism**. A key is a set of questions. Answering one question divides a group of organisms into smaller groups. Each question leads to another question until each organism is named. Using a key makes it easier to understand how and why animals are grouped together.

The branching key

There are many different kinds of keys used by scientists. One of the most popular is called a branching key. A branching key looks like a tree branch. As a tree branch goes from larger branches to smaller branches, and then to twigs, the key goes from larger groups of organisms into smaller groups, until it reaches one **species**. This type of simple key is sometimes called a **dichotomous** key. This just means that each question in the key divides one group into two.

Using a key

Below is an example of a simple branching key. This branching key will break this group of four animals into individual species by asking questions.

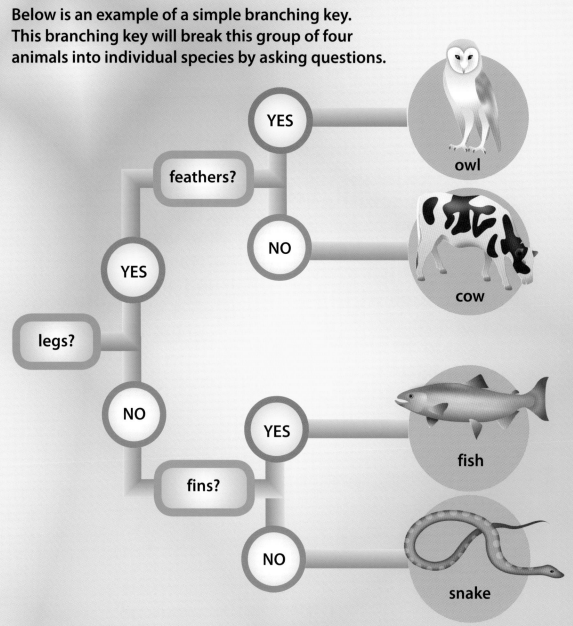

Notice how each question in the key breaks a group of animals into two groups, until each animal is identified. When a new species of animal is discovered, scientists may use a key like this, although much larger, to determine how the new animal should be classified. Questions like this are answered so the creature can be put in a **kingdom** then a **phylum**, **class**, **order**, **family**, **genus**, and finally an individual species.

DETERMINE THE DINOSAUR!

Even though dinosaurs are extinct, they are considered to be part of the animal kingdom. Dinosaurs are actually believed by scientists to be closely related to birds that live today. You can use this dinosaur key to determine which picture belongs to which species of dinosaur. You should be able to look at the pictures and answer the questions in the key. If you do this carefully you will be able to identify which species each of these dinosaurs belongs to. You can check your answers on page 47 of this book.

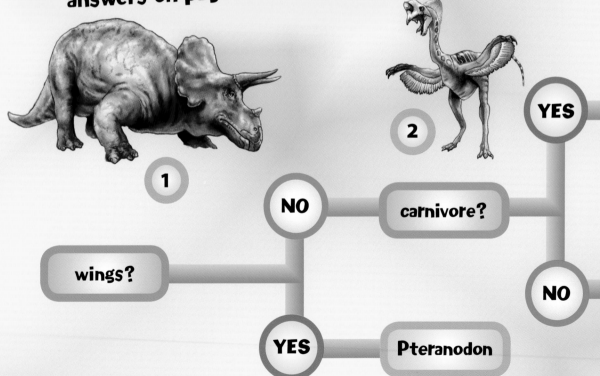

1

2

YES

NO

carnivore?

wings?

NO

YES

Pteranodon

A key to classifying dinosaurs

Take a look at each of the dinosaur pictures. Now study the branching key diagram. Can you match up the correct name to each dinosaur?

5

3

4

YES — Oviraptor

feathers?

NO — Tyrannosaurus Rex

YES — Triceratops

horned head?

NO — Apatosaurus

ANIMAL KINGDOM

The animal **kingdom** contains over a million known **species** and possibly millions more that scientists have not yet discovered. Some scientists estimate that when all of the species of animals in places like the tropical rainforest and deep in the ocean are discovered, the number of animals will be over 10 million species!

The first animals many people think of are common animals like the cat, horse, or dog. However, the animal kingdom includes a very diverse group of creatures. There are insects, fish, and birds in the animal kingdom as well!

You probably already knew that a bear was part of the animal kingdom. Did you know that fish are too?

What makes an animal?

Some of the most important things that make a species a part of the animal kingdom are:

- They can usually move from place to place
- Their bodies are made up of many **cells**
- They usually reproduce sexually
- They eat other living things
- They don't have rigid (hard) cell walls (plants have rigid cell walls).

Phyla of the animal kingdom

There are 33 phyla in the animal kingdom. Phyla is the plural of the word **phylum**. Remember that phylum is the level just below kingdom in the **Linnaean classification system**.

Kingdom
Phylum
Class
Order
Family
Genus
Species

Vertebrates and invertebrates

The animal kingdom can be split into two main groups. If you run your fingers down your back, the bumpy bones you feel make up your backbone. That means you are a **vertebrate**. The animal kingdom is grouped into **invertebrates** (without a backbone) and vertebrates (with a backbone). Invertebrates make up 97 per cent of animals.

Invertebrates

There are more than a million **invertebrates**. They range from a simple sponge found in the ocean to millions of insects found almost everywhere on Earth. Remember that invertebrates include all animals without backbones. There are snails, squid, worms, crabs, coral, and many, many more. So how do scientists classify all of these **species**?

Breaking down invertebrates

Scientists look at further characteristics to break down the invertebrates and give them each a specific name. Some of the characteristics that they use to break down the invertebrates are body structure, what they eat, where they live, how they move, and how they reproduce.

Some of the major phyla of the invertebrates

KEY
> = greater than
< = less than

Phylum	Some things it includes	Estimate number
Annelida	segmented worms like earthworms and leeches	>15,000
Arthropoda	centipedes, spiders, lobsters, and insects	>1 million
Nematoda	roundworms	>15,000
Echinodermata	starfish, sea cucumbers, sand dollars, and sea urchins	>7,000
Cnidaria	jellyfish and corals	>9,000
Mollusca	molluscs, snails, slugs, octopuses, and squid	>100,000
Platyhelminthes	flatworms	>25,000
Porifera	sponges	>5,000
Nematomorpha	horsehair worms or gordian worms	>300

Did you know?

- If a starfish loses an arm, it can actually grow another one!

- A common cockroach can live for a week without its head. It eventually dies because of dehydration.

23

Phyla of invertebrates

Let's take a closer look at some of the different **phylum** of invertebrates and the characteristics that scientists use to classify them.

Insecta

Insects are in the phylum Insecta. Insects have bodies divided into three sections. They have three pairs of legs and some can have one or two pairs of wings.

Porifera

Sponges are in the phylum Porifera. Sponges don't have mouths. Instead water goes through their **pores** (small holes) and food is filtered out. Most of them are small, but some can grow to 1.8 metres (6 feet) long!

Cnidaria

Jellyfish, sea anemones, and corals are in the phylum Cnidaria. Their body shape is made up of a single soft sac. They have **tentacles** (long, narrow strands that hang down around their mouths) and stinging cells. They feed on prey that their tentacles sting.

Jellyfish are beautiful members of the Cnidaria phylum. But watch out — 70 species of jellyfish are known to sting. Some can even kill a human!

Mollusca

Snails, slugs, clams, mussels, octopuses, and squid are in the phylum Mollusca. They have soft bodies. Some are protected in a hard shell. Others are not but protect themselves in different ways, such as spraying dark ink or hiding in small spaces. Most are found in a water environment.

An octopus is a well known invertebrate in the Mollusca phylum. They don't have hard shells but are very good at hiding. Some can make themselves look like other animals!

Echinodermata

Starfish, sea cucumbers, sand dollars, and sea urchins are in the phylum Echinodermata. Their name means "spiny-skinned". They have rays or arms in multiples of five, and sucker-tubed feet. They use them to stick to rocks and move across the sea floor.

Worms

This leech is a bloodsucker! It attaches itself to much larger animals and will drink blood. When it's full, the leech falls off the animal.

Worms include flatworms, tapeworms, roundworms, earthworms, leeches, marine worms, and others. Worms have long, soft, legless bodies. They lack brains, but have nerve centres that control them.

Arthropoda

The arthropod **phylum** includes **classes** such as insecta, arachnida, and crustacea. They have special features that make them part of the **Arthropoda** phylum including:

- **segmented (divided into sections) bodies**
- **arms or legs on at least one segment**
- **exoskeletons (hard outer skeleton) which protect their soft bodies**
- **two antennae**
- **jointed legs.**

There are many different animals in each phylum. Scientists break down the phyla even further and group animals into classes.

Insects

Insects are in the class Insecta. Their three main body parts are the head, the thorax (middle part), and the abdomen (rear part). They have compound eyes, which are made up of hundreds of tiny, separate visual units, and six legs. Most have wings to fly and antennae to smell and taste. They live all over the world, and some have a life span of just 24 hours!

Crustaceans

Crab, lobsters, barnacles, water fleas, shrimp, and woodlice are in the class Crustacea. Some crustaceans have very strong claws. They are used for protection. The coconut crab is the largest invertebrate at 17 kilograms (37.5 pounds).

Centipedes

Centipedes are from the class Chilopoda. They live on land in moist climates. They are worm-like and have a flattened body. Centipedes have poisonous bites! You should never handle a centipede.

In Latin, *centi* means 100 and *pedis* means foot. So centipede means "100 feet". They don't have quite that many!

Arachnids

Spiders, scorpions, ticks, and mites make up the class Arachnida. Their bodies are divided into two parts and they have eight legs. They do not have antennae or wings. Scorpions have venomous (poisonous) stings in their tails used for self-defence and to capture prey.

Scorpions are in the class Arachnid. They can have 6 to 12 eyes!

CLASSIFICATION AND EVOLUTION

When the **Linnaean classification system** was developed, the theory of **evolution** (that new **species** arise from old species) was not widely accepted. As evolution has been accepted by scientists, classification has been used to identify common ancestors of species. This also allows scientists to determine which animals are the most closely related.

Phylogeny trees

A phylogeny tree is a diagram of the "tree of life". It is a way to show that all living things are related to each other. It also shows which are the most closely related.

This is a branch from a phylogeny tree. Look at the branch carefully. Can you guess which animal on this branch is the most closely related to humans?

mouse

human

birds

fish

common ancestor

If you said that the mouse is the most closely related of these three animals you were right! All of these animals evolved from a common ancestor. You can see that humans and mice remained on the same branch longer than birds or fish. This just means that the mouse and human have a more recent common ancestor.

Determining relatedness

When scientists begin to classify an unknown organism they look for common features. However, scientists have to be careful when determining **homologies** from **analogies**.

- Homologies: when two animals have a similar feature they **inherited** from a common ancestor. An example is the front legs of a frog and a rabbit. Both inherited their front legs from the same ancestor.
- Analogies: features that appear common between two animals but were not inherited from a common ancestor. The wings of a bird and a bat are analogies. They appear similar but developed independently. They did not inherit them from the same ancestor.

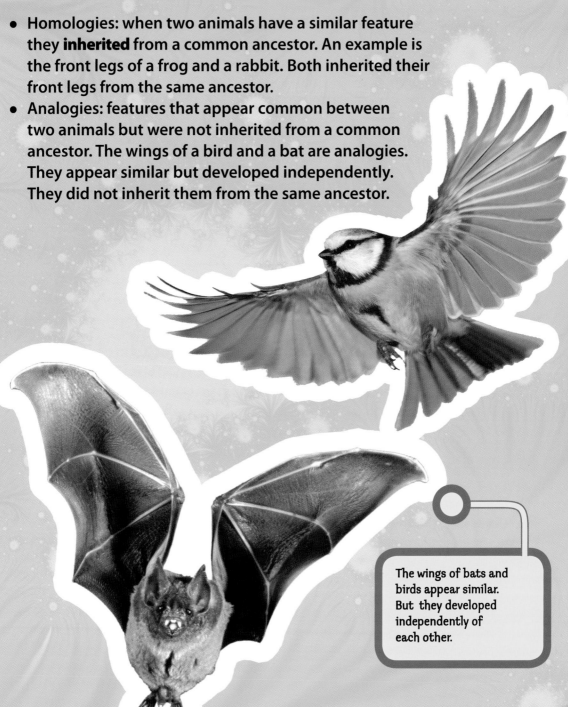

The wings of bats and birds appear similar. But they developed independently of each other.

DNA
AND CLASSIFICATION

Every living thing contains DNA. <u>DNA are tiny stores of genetic information found in all animal species. This is the information that parents pass on to their offspring.</u> Species that are related have similar DNA. The ability to analyze DNA has made classification a more exact science.

Classification was created to identify and group species using traits scientists could see. If the differences or similarities between two organisms were not easy to see, scientists would have difficulty grouping them.

Now scientists can decide how closely related organisms are by looking at their DNA. This allows species to be grouped much more accurately than before. Let's look at a few examples of how DNA analysis has led scientists to new discoveries in the classification of animals.

Humans and chimps

It was recently found that chimpanzees have DNA that is 99.4 per cent the same as humans. This is higher than any other species of animal. This means that humans and chimps are much more closely related than scientists originally thought. In fact, some scientists are arguing that chimpanzees should be regrouped into the same genus as human beings!

Elephants can weigh up to 12,000 kg (26,000 lb)!

The hyrax is a close relative of the elephant. However, it only weighs 2–5 kg (4.5–11 lb).

Unexpected relatives

Based on DNA analysis and physical evidence, scientists now think that the hyrax is one of the closest living relatives of today's elephants! About 50–60 million years ago, pig-sized mammals were the ancestors to both the hyrax and elephant. A hyrax is a chubby, furry mammal with a stubby tail. From a distance the animal could be mistaken for a large rabbit, but not an elephant! It is incredible to think that such different-looking animals could be so closely related!

THE VERTEBRATES

You have already learned about many **invertebrates** in this book. However, when most people think of animals they think mainly of **vertebrates**. Alligators, birds, fish, humans, and many other **species** are all vertebrates. Nearly 60,000 types of vertebrates have been classified.

What makes a vertebrate?

All vertebrates have a backbone that is made up of a series of bones. These bones, called the vertebrae, surround the spinal cord. The spinal cord and brain work together to control everything in the animal's body. They also have an **internal** skeleton that protects vital **organs**, such as the heart and lungs. It also allows the animal to move.

Breaking down vertebrates

Scientists look at further characteristics to group the vertebrates and give them each a specific name. Some of the characteristics that they use to break down the vertebrates are body structure, what they eat, where they live, how they move, and how they reproduce. Let's look at two of the major ways the vertebrates are grouped.

What they eat

One characteristic that scientists use to group vertebrates is their diets. The major groupings are:

- **Herbivores**: eat mostly plants
- **Carnivores**: eat mostly meat
- **Omnivores**: eat both plants and meat.

Body temperature

Body temperature is another characteristic used. The major groupings are:

- **Cold-blooded**: an animal whose internal body temperature adjusts to match the external temperature of the environment. Fish, amphibians, and reptiles are cold-blooded animals.
- **Warm-blooded**: an animal that controls its body temperature. Humans are warm-blooded. No matter what temperature it is outside, our internal body temperature remains the same.

The alligator is a cold-blooded carnivore!

Classes of vertebrates

We have already looked at the animal kingdom. The Chordata phylum groups together all animals with a similar body plan. Remember, as we move down the list of classification levels, each level gets smaller and more specific.

There are seven **classes** of vertebrates in the animal kingdom. Three of these include only fish. The others include amphibians, reptiles, birds, and mammals.

Kingdom	Animalia
Phylum	Chordata
Class	**7 classes of vertebrates**
Order	
Family	
Genus	
Species	

Amphibians

Amphibians are a class of cold-blooded vertebrates. They have smooth, scaleless skin and four limbs. The adults breathe through lungs and their moist skin. Their young breathe through gills, like fish.

Amphibians are the only animals that go through **metamorphosis**. This means they have a dramatic change in form. For instance, when a baby frog changes from a tadpole to a frog, it goes through metamorphosis.

The axolotl is also a strange exception to the amphibian class! Axolotls never go through metamorphosis. The adults keep their gills and spend their entire lives in the water!

Frogs and toads

Frogs and toads are the most common examples of amphibians. They may look almost the same, but there are big differences. Frogs have bulging eyes, long, webbed hind feet for leaping and swimming, and slimy skin. Frogs also lay eggs in clusters. Toads have stubby bodies, short hind legs for walking, bumpy dry skin, and poison glands behind their eyes. Toads lay eggs in long chains. Frogs and toads eat insects.

The fire-bellied toad

Scientific name: *Bombina bombina*

Class: Amphibia

Location: Europe and Asia

Size: 4–7 cm (1.6–2.8 in) in length

Interesting fact: Fire-bellied toads give off a poison that makes them taste horrible to their predators Their red belly is a poison warning.

This tadpole is in the process of metamorphosis. it is slowly becoming a frog.

Orders of reptiles

Now let's look at the **order** level of classification. This level is even more specific than class.

Kingdom	Animalia
Phylum	Chordata
Class	Reptilia
Order	**4 orders of reptiles**
Family	
Genus	
Species	

Reptiles

The class of reptiles includes air-breathing, cold-blooded vertebrates. They have scaly skin and four limbs. Reptiles lay eggs with tough, leathery shells. They must be in the Sun to get warm and move out of the Sun to cool down.

There are four orders of the reptile class. Each of these orders is very specific. For instance, the order Crocodilia contains crocodiles and alligators. The others include:

- Order Testudinata – turtles
- Order Rhynchocephalia – tuatara (an animal that looks like a lizard)
- Order Squamata – snakes and lizards.

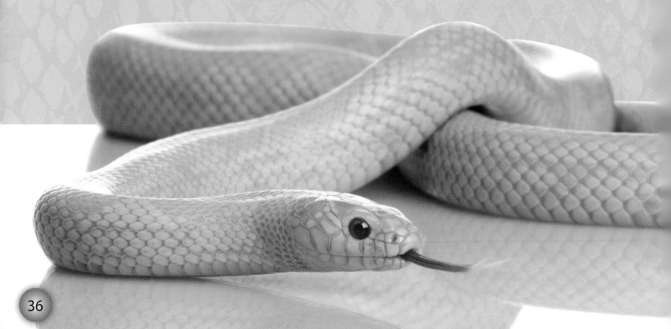

The Squamata order

The Squamata order of reptiles contains snakes and lizards. All snakes are carnivores. They eat other animals. They can dislocate their jaw if the animal is too big to fit in their mouth! Lizards have four legs and can be found in all different climates. They can range in size from the tiny dwarf gecko, which is only 1.6 centimetres (0.6 inches) long, to the gigantic Komodo dragon, which can reach 3 metres (10 feet) and weigh 166 kilograms (366 pounds)!

Snakes can smell with their tongues. When a snake sticks out its tongue it smells its surroundings.

Amazing animals

The Gila monster

Scientific name: *Heloderma suspectum*

Order: Squamata

Location: southwestern United States and Mexico

Size: 60 cm (2.0 ft) in length

Interesting fact: The Gila monster is the only poisonous lizard in the United States. Its venom is a neurotoxin as toxic as that of a diamondback rattlesnake!

Families of birds

Below the order level of classification is the **family** level. On the last page we saw that the order Crocodilia contains both crocodiles and alligators. However, at the family level, these groups are separated into the more specific Crocodylidae and Alligatoridae families.

Kingdom	Animalia
Phylum	Chordata
Class	**Aves** (Birds)
Order	23 orders of birds
Family	**Over 200 families of birds**
Genus	
Species	

Birds

Birds are warm-blooded vertebrates. Some scientists think that birds are descendants of dinosaurs! They have scales on their legs, feathers, wings, and beaks. Birds that eat animals have strong, hooked-shaped beaks. Those that eat nuts have short, thick, curved beaks. Some birds eat plant nectar, and their beaks are long like straws.

The kiwi is the only bird with nostrils at the end of its beak. it has a highly developed sense of smell.

Amazing animals

The emperor penguin

Scientific name: *Aptenodytes forsteri*

Family: Spheniscidae

Location: Antarctica

Size: 122 cm (48 in) in length

Interesting fact: The emperor penguin is the largest species of penguin. It weighs 22–37 kg (48–82 lb).

Ostriches don't really hide their heads in the sand. They bury their eggs in the sand and occasionally move them around with their beaks.

Flightless birds

There are about 40 species of flightless birds. These birds cannot fly. Instead, they run or swim. Flightless birds have more feathers than flying birds. Penguins, rheas, emus, kiwis, and cassowaries are flightless birds.

The heaviest and tallest bird that exists is a flightless bird. It is the ostrich. It can run as fast as a racehorse! The ostrich is in the family Struthionidae. It is the only living member of this family. Families are very specific and usually very small. Often they only contain one species!

Genus of mammals

The final level of classification containing multiple species is the **genus**. To be in the same genus animals must be very closely related. Usually animals that are not part of the same species cannot produce offspring together. However, in some special circumstances, different species of the same genus may be able to.

Kingdom	Animalia
Phylum	Chordata
Class	Mammalia
Order	29 orders of mammals
Family	Over 150 families of mammals
Genus	**About 1,200 genera of mammals**
Species	

Mammals

Mammals are a class of warm-blooded vertebrate that breathe air through their lungs. They are the only animals that produce milk for their young, and care for them until they are old enough to survive alone. There are mammals that live in the water, such as the whale, and mammals that live on land. You are a mammal, too!

Amazing animals

The bumblebee bat

Scientific name: *Craseonycteris thonglongyai*

Genus: *Craseonycteris*

Location: Thailand and Burma

Size: 29–33 millimetres (1.14–1.30 inches) in length

Interesting fact: The world's smallest mammal, the bumblebee bat is the size of a jellybean. It has a pig-like snout and can hover in the air like a hummingbird.

There are about 1,200 genera (plural of genus) of mammals. Some of these contain several living species and some contain only one or less.

The *Equus* family

The *Equus* genus is a group of horse-like animals. It includes only horses, donkeys, and zebras. These animals are all very closely related. In fact, these animals have been successfully able to produce offspring together. A mule is a cross of a horse and a donkey. A mix between a horse and a zebra is called a zorse!

A horse and a zebra are so closely related that they can produce offspring! However, mules and zorses cannot produce offspring of their own.

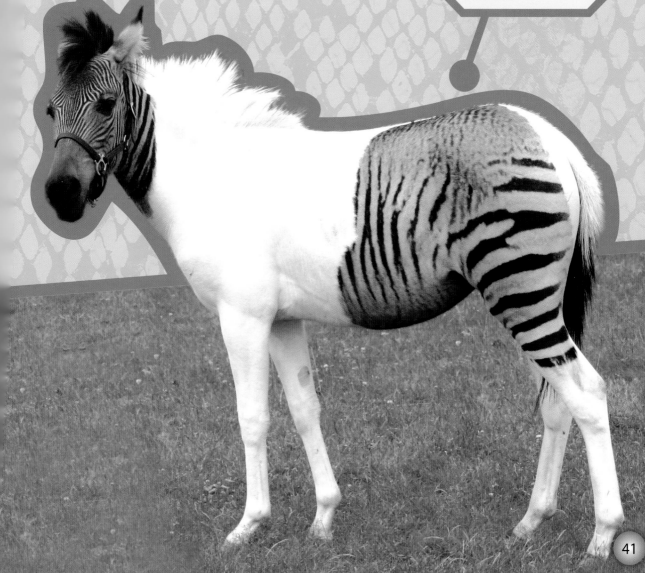

Discovering new species

Scientists are discovering more new **species** in the 21st century than in any other time in history. New technology allows people to search new areas, like deep within the ocean, remote areas in the rainforest, or on high mountain tops. Believe it or not, most of Earth's species haven't even been identified yet!

Newly discovered species:

2002

Scientists discover two new primates in the deep rainforests of South Central Amazon. They place them in the **genus** *Callicebus*. They are cat-sized titi monkeys with sideburns. (See photo to the right.)

2003

Japanese scientists discover a new species of whale! It is 12 m (40 ft) long! The name for the new whale is *Balaenoptera omurai*.

2004

Scientists detect 1,800 new species of microbes by studying a single water sample from the Sargasso Sea. There must be millions of tiny species we don't even know about yet!

Classifying new species

Sometimes scientists can use **DNA** evidence, as well as comparing the common characteristics of new species with previously known species, to group the new species into already established **families**. However, there are also many new species for which scientists will need to create whole new groups!

Callicebus stephennashi, one of the two new species of titi monkey.

2005

Scientists discover a new species of marine worm. This worm lives in whale bones on the sea floor. They name the species *Osedax mucofloris*, meaning "bone-eating snot flower".

A team of scientists in New Guinea discover dozens of new species. One of the discoveries was a golden-mantled tree kangaroo.

2008

Scientists discover a bowling-ball-sized fossil frog in Madagascar. They name the frog *Beelzebufo ampinga*, meaning "armoured devil toad".

Summary

Classification, then and now

- Scientists around the world name and group animals with one system, the Linnaean classification system.
- Scientists have used mainly their eyes to determine which animals appear to have the most common features.
- Recently, DNA analysis has allowed scientists to classify with greater accuracy than was previously possible.

Seven levels of classification

- Kingdom: The highest level contains all animals. The levels get more and more specific as they drop down.
- Phylum
- Class
- Order
- Family
- Genus: A group of species that share one or more characteristics. The first word in the scientific name is the genus. The first letter is always capitalized.
- Species: The smallest group. Members of a species can reproduce together.

The two-part name given to each animal is based on the animal's genus and species. The genus and species are the most specific groups that any animal belongs to, and thus are used to name the animal.

A simple key to classifying

Remember that a simple branching key is a set of questions that can be used to classify and group any number of living things. The questions of a branching key have to be specific. This allows for each living thing to be identified as unique and given a unique name.

Can you remember?

What small, furry animal is closely related to a giant elephant?
(hint: see page 31)
Who was the Swedish scientist who came up with a famous method for classifying animals?
(hint: see pages 6–7)
True or false: over 97 per cent of all animals are vertebrates?
(hint: see page 21)
What kind of animal that is common today might be descended from dinosaurs?
(hint: see page 38)

Glossary

algae   plant-like organism that makes its own food and is part of the protist kingdom

analogies   features (such as wings) that have the same form or function in different species but have no known common ancestor

animalia   kingdom of living things that includes all animals. They are multi-cellular organisms that ingest food.

archaea   single-celled organisms that are found in extreme environments, such as hot springs

arthropoda   animal phylum consisting of creatures that have external skeletons, and jointed bodies and limbs.

autotroph   organism that produces its own food. Plants are autotrophs.

aves   class of vertebrates that includes all birds

bacteria   single-celled organisms capable of all life functions. Scientists believe that bacteria were the first living things on Earth.

carnivores   mostly meat-eating animals

cell   basic unit of life

cellulose   carbohydrate that forms the hard cell wall in most plants

class   level of classification in the Linnaean classification system. Humans are members of the class Mammalia.

cold-blooded   animals whose bodies adjust to the temperature of the environment around them

dichotomous key   key consisting of a series of questions that, when answered, lead the user to the correct species. It is also known as a branching key.

DNA   tiny strands of genetic information in all animal species

eubacteria   kingdom of single-celled micro-organisms

evolution   theory that new species arise from old species

exoskeleton   hard supporting or protective structure (as of an insect, spider, or crustacean) on the outside of the body

family   one of the more specific levels of classification

fungi   any of numerous plant-like organisms of the kingdom Fungi. Most feed off of dead plants and animals.

genus (plural **genera**)   group of closely related species. In the Linnaean classification system, genus is the category immediately above species.

herbivores   animals that eat mostly plants

homologies   anatomical structures in different species that were inherited from a common ancestor

inherit   to receive a characteristic from a parent or common ancestor

internal   inside of the body

45

invertebrate animal that lacks an internal skeleton and backbone. About 97 per cent of all animals are invertebrates.

kingdom highest level of classification. Kingdom Animalia contains all animals.

Linnaean classification system referring to the classification system in use by the biological sciences today to classify all living things. It was invented by Carl Linnaeus in the 18th century.

metamorphosis changing of certain animals from one stage of development to another, such as when a tadpole begins to change into a frog

multi-cellular having more than one cell

neocortex region part of the brain that only mammals have

omnivore animal that eats both plants and animals

order Linnaean classification category above the level of species and genus and below class

organ part of the body that performs a certain function, such as the brain. An organ is made up of more than one kind of tissue.

organism living thing

phylogeny trees trees of life. These show evolutionary relationships between species.

phylum (plural **phyla**) level of classification just below kingdom in the Linnaean Classification system

plants kingdom of plants in the Linnaean slassification system. Members of this kingdom produce food and energy from inorganic material by photosynthesis.

pores small holes. There are pores on your skin.

protists single-celled organisms including algae and protozoa. Protist cells have a nucleus.

protozoa any of a group of tiny animals that are single-celled protists and have varied structure

single-celled organism living thing made up of only one cell

species single group of animals considered to be the same based on their ability to reproduce together

taxonomy science of classification

tentacle long, narrow, and movable strands that form around the mouth or head of some invertebrates. Squid and jellyfish have tentacles.

tissue group of the same type of cells that do a job together

vertebrates animals that possess a spinal cord protected by a vertebral column

warm-blooded animals that maintain a relatively constant core body temperature regardless of environmental conditions

Find out more

Books

Animals: Multicelled Life, Robert Sneddon (Heinemann Library, 2008)

Animals Under Threat, Richard and Louise Spilsbury (Heinemann Library, 2007)

Life Science in Depth: Variation and Classification, Ann Fullick (Heinemann Library, 2008)

Websites

http://www.hhmi.org/coolscience/forkids/critters/critters.html
Interactive site that allows you to classify animals.

http://www.zsl.org/zsl-london-zoo/animals/
Find out information about different animals on London Zoo's website.

http://coolcosmos.ipac.caltech.edu/image_galleries/ir_zoo/
The infrared zoo. See what animals look like through thermal infrared cameras.

http://www.bbc.co.uk/schools/ks3bitesize/science/biology/classification_intro.shtml
This site gives basic information on classification.

http://microbeworld.org/microbes/bacteria/default.aspx
Go here for information on bacteria and other tiny organisms.

Answers from page 18–19

1. Triceratops **2.** Oviraptor **3.** Apatosaurus **4.** *Tyrannosaurus Rex* **5.** Pteranodon

Index